Kimchi Diet for Women

A Beginner's Step-by-Step Guide on How to Make it at Home, With Sample Kimchi Recipes and an Overview of its Use Cases

mf

copyright © 2022 Isadora Kwon

All rights reserved No part of this book may be reproduced, or stored in a retrieval system, or transmitted in any form or by any means, electronic, mechanical, photocopying, recording, or otherwise, without express written permission of the publisher.

Disclaimer

By reading this disclaimer, you are accepting the terms of the disclaimer in full. If you disagree with this disclaimer, please do not read the guide.

All of the content within this guide is provided for informational and educational purposes only, and should not be accepted as independent medical or other professional advice. The author is not a doctor, physician, nurse, mental health provider, or registered nutritionist/dietician. Therefore, using and reading this guide does not establish any form of a physician-patient relationship.

Always consult with a physician or another qualified health provider with any issues or questions you might have regarding any sort of medical condition. Do not ever disregard any qualified professional medical advice or delay seeking that advice because of anything you have read in this guide. The information in this guide is not intended to be any sort of medical advice and should not be used in lieu of any medical advice by a licensed and qualified medical professional.

The information in this guide has been compiled from a variety of known sources. However, the author cannot attest to or guarantee the accuracy of each source and thus should not be held liable for any errors or omissions.

You acknowledge that the publisher of this guide will not be held liable for any loss or damage of any kind incurred as a result of this guide or the reliance on any information provided within this guide. You acknowledge and agree that you assume all risk and responsibility for any action you undertake in response to the information in this guide.

Using this guide does not guarantee any particular result (e.g., weight loss or a cure). By reading this guide, you acknowledge that there are no guarantees to any specific outcome or results you can expect.

All product names, diet plans, or names used in this guide are for identification purposes only and are the property of their respective owners. The use of these names does not imply endorsement. All other trademarks cited herein are the property of their respective owners.

Where applicable, this guide is not intended to be a substitute for the original work of this diet plan and is, at most, a supplement to the original work for this diet plan and never a direct substitute. This guide is a personal expression of the facts of that diet plan.

Where applicable, persons shown in the cover images are stock photography models and the publisher has obtained the rights to use the images through license agreements with third-party stock image companies.

Table of Contents

Introduction   6
    What is Kimchi?   8
    Kimchi Nutrition Facts   9
Background and History of Kimchi   12
    What is the Kimchi Diet?   13
    Health Benefits of Kimchi   15
Use Cases of Kimchi for Health   18
Health Benefits of Kimchi for Women   22
    Potential Risks or Side Effects of Eating Kimchi   24
8-Step Guide to Making Kimchi at Home   26
3-Step Guide on How to Incorporate Kimchi Into Your Diet   30
Sample Recipes of Kimchi Dishes   32
    Kimchi Fried Rice   33
    Kimchi Pancakes   35
    Spicy Kimchi Noodles   37
    Kimchi Soup   39
    Braised Pork with Kimchi   40
    Korean Kimchi Chicken   42
    Kimchi Fried Egg   44
    Kimchi Quesadilla   45
    Kimchi Grilled Cheese Sandwich   47
    Kimchi Dumplings Recipe   49
Conclusion   51
FAQ   54
References and Helpful Links   56

Introduction

Over the last several years, there has been an increasing interest in the impact that nutrition plays on the health of women. For many years, the golden rule of nutrition has been to consume a well-rounded diet that features lots of fresh fruit and vegetables. On the other hand, this strategy has come under growing scrutiny as a result of new research which suggests that some foods may have a stronger influence on the health of women than others.

The so-called "kimchi diet" is one of the most notable examples available today. Fermented vegetables like kimchi are a focal point of this diet, which is quite common in Korea. According to the findings of a few pieces of research, the process of fermenting these veggies may make them less difficult to digest and absorb, in addition to the possibility that they offer more health advantages than other kinds of vegetables.

In addition, the kimchi diet incorporates a wide variety of other nutritious foods, like rice, salmon, and other items made from soy. As a consequence of this, it is possible that adhering to a kimchi diet is a more efficient strategy for enhancing women's health than the more conventional method of adhering to a balanced diet.

Even though further study is required to back up these claims, the kimchi diet is just one of the many new dietary methods that are beginning to gain favor among women who are looking to enhance their health by making adjustments to the foods they eat.

In this introduction to kimchi and the kimchi diet, we are going to focus on the following subtopics for a more in-depth discussion:

- What is kimchi?
- Kimchi nutrition facts
- Background and history of kimchi
- What is the kimchi diet
- Health benefits of kimchi
- Use cases of kimchi for health
- Health benefits of kimchi for women
- Potential risks and side effects of eating kimchi
- 8-step guide to making kimchi at home
- Sample recipes of kimchi dishes

So, read on and discover the many health benefits of a kimchi diet for women!

What is Kimchi?

Fermented kimchi is an excellent source of essential nutrients including vitamins A, B, and C, as well as minerals like iron and calcium. Additionally, it includes phytochemicals and antioxidants, both of which contribute to the promotion of numerous health advantages. The amount of heat in kimchi might vary, but in general, it is rather spicy. This Korean delicacy is most commonly prepared and served as a side dish; however, it may also be utilized in the preparation of stews, soups, and stir-fries.

There are a variety of veggies that may be used to make kimchi, including radishes, carrots, cucumbers, Napa cabbage, and scallions, among others. It pairs well with a variety of spices, including ginger, garlic, chili peppers, and others.

Kimchi undergoes fermentation, which can take anywhere from one to two days at ambient temperature but moves more slowly when stored in the refrigerator. For food safety reasons, kimchi should be stored in the refrigerator whenever possible. When the fermentation process is complete, the liquid will either start to smell sour or you will notice bubbles in the liquid. During the fermentation process of kimchi, lactic acid bacteria grow and create carbon dioxide; this is the likely cause of any bubbles that may appear. The fermentation process results in the production of helpful probiotics, which are important for the health of the digestive tract.

The fermenting process of producing kimchi can take several weeks, and the completed product has a shelf life of up to six months if it is kept in the refrigerator. When you go to the store to buy kimchi, make sure to seek jars that are labeled "vegan" or "gluten-free." The fermenting process of certain brands may involve the addition of fish or shellfish.

Kimchi Nutrition Facts

Kimchi is packed with nutrients and minerals. Below are the primary nutrients found in kimchi, according to nutrition-value.org.

Vitamin A: Vitamin A, also known as retinol, is a fat-soluble vitamin that plays an important role in maintaining healthy eyesight as well as reproductive and immunological systems. Approximately 18% of the Daily Value (DV) for vitamin A may be found in a serving size of kimchi that is equivalent to one cup (150 grams).

Calorie: The term "calorie" refers to a unit of measurement for energy. There are just 23 calories in a serving size of kimchi which is equal to one cup (150 grams).

Fat: There is just 1 gram of fat in a serving size of kimchi which is equal to 1 cup (150 grams).

Protein: There are 2 grams of protein in a serving size of kimchi which is equal to 1 cup (150 grams).

Carbs: There are 4 grams of carbohydrates in a serving size of kimchi which is equal to 1 cup (150 grams).

Fiber: A serving of kimchi containing 1 cup (150 grams) provides 2 grams of fiber, which is equivalent to 8% of the daily value.

Vitamin C: Vitamin C is a water-soluble vitamin that plays a crucial role in the recovery of wounds, the formation of bones, and the operation of the immune system. Approximately 22% of the daily value for vitamin C is included in a serving of kimchi that is equal to 1 cup (or 150 grams).

Vitamin B6: Vitamin B6 is a water-soluble vitamin that plays a crucial role in the synthesis of red blood cells, as well as in the maintenance and operation of the immune system and metabolism. There is approximately 19% of the daily value for vitamin B6 in a serving of kimchi that is equal to one cup (or 150 grams).

Folate: Folate is a water-soluble vitamin that is required for the production of DNA and the division of cells. Folate is needed. There is around 20% of the daily value for folate in a serving of kimchi that is equal to one cup (or 150 grams).

Iron: Iron is a mineral that plays a crucial role in the transportation of oxygen and the generation of electricity. Approximately 21% of the daily value for iron is included in a serving of kimchi that is equal to 1 cup (or 150 grams).

Potassium*:* Potassium is a mineral that plays an important role in maintaining the body's fluid and muscle balance. Potassium is required for normal muscular function. Approximately 5% of the daily value for potassium is included in a serving of kimchi that is equal to 1 cup (or 150 grams).

Calcium*:* Calcium is a mineral that plays an important role in maintaining healthy bones and proper muscular function. Approximately 4% of the daily value for calcium may be found in a serving of kimchi that is equal to one cup (or 150 grams).

Background and History of Kimchi

The cold weather that early Korean farmers had to endure made it difficult for them to be successful in their pursuits. The most frequent strategy for storing food for the next winter was to use salt as a preservative for a variety of different meals.

The oldest records of the Korean people's competence in food preservation date back to the era of the Three Kingdoms, which was a significant amount of time before the present nation-state of Korea was formally created.

The first written references to kimchi come from the Goryeo period of Korean history. During this period, there was a significant rise in the amount of trade that took place between Korea and other kingdoms, and new crops, such as napa or Chinese cabbage, were brought into the country. Because of this, the methods for preparing kimchi have developed greatly throughout time. In the beginning, radishes were used to produce kimchi since they were easily accessible. However, as the dish developed over the years, additional vegetables and spices were ultimately incorporated into its composition.

There is an abundance of different kinds of kimchi that may be purchased today.

The traditional Korean side dish known as kimchi has been adapted into dozens of different forms over the previous two centuries. There are over two hundred different kinds of kimchi that may be purchased right now. Because of its versatility, kimchi has emerged as one of the most well-liked condiments and side dishes in cuisines all over the world.

Among the various forms of kimchi are chonggak kimchi, mul kimchi (water kimchi), and kkakdugi (cubed radish kimchi) (ponytail radish kimchi). Kimchi is an essential component in a wide variety of traditional Korean dishes, including kimchi fried rice, kimchi pancakes, kimchi stew, and spicy pork stir fry, to name just a few.

What is the Kimchi Diet?

A traditional Korean meal prepared from fermented cabbage, kimchi is the centerpiece of the kimchi diet, which is a weight-loss strategy that centers on the eating of kimchi. The diet is predicated on the idea that kimchi can aid in the process of speeding up the metabolism and shedding excess fat. There are also claims made by supporters of the diet that consuming kimchi can assist to improve digestion and create a healthy microbiota in the stomach.

Despite the absence of any proof from scientific research to back up these assertions, the kimchi diet has been gaining popularity over the past few years. Because it is low in calories and contains a high concentration of nutrients, kimchi is an ideal food to include in any diet that focuses on weight loss.

Additionally, because of the fermenting process, kimchi is both simple to digest and abundant in probiotics, both of which are good for the health of the digestive tract. For these reasons, those who are interested in healthily losing weight might think about trying the kimchi diet.

The key to the success of the kimchi diet is to substitute kimchi for high-calorie meals. You may, for instance, opt to have a bowl of kimchi for lunch rather than a hamburger for that meal. The proponents of the plan assert that eating kimchi can assist you in losing weight by revving up your metabolism and causing your body to burn more fat. In addition, they assert that regular consumption of kimchi can facilitate better digestion and contribute to the maintenance of healthy microbiota in the gut. Nevertheless, there is not a single piece of scientific data to back up these statements.

The majority of individuals can follow the kimchi diet without risk. On the other hand, it is essential to be aware that the fermenting process might cause certain varieties of kimchi to have a significant amount of salt. Before beginning the kimchi diet, it is important to see your primary care physician if you have high blood pressure, are on a diet that limits the amount of salt you consume, or are pregnant or nursing.

Health Benefits of Kimchi

Consuming kimchi may provide a host of advantageous health effects, particularly in the digestive system. These advantages are mostly attributable to the fermenting process as well as the unusual concoction of components that can be discovered in kimchi.

Rich in vitamins and minerals*:* Research has shown that eating kimchi regularly can help increase immunity, improve digestion, and even reduce the risk of developing cancer. Kimchi is rich in vitamins A, C, and K. In addition, kimchi is packed with a wide range of nutrients, including calcium, magnesium, and iron, among others. These nutrients are necessary for the preservation of good health, and they have been shown to assist in the enhancement of energy levels, the reduction of stress, and the promotion of bone and joint health.

Contains probiotics*:* The fermenting process that kimchi undergoes results in the production of probiotics. Probiotics are good bacteria that can aid in the improvement of gastrointestinal health. These bacteria contribute to the process of digesting food, extracting nutrients, and producing vitamins, all of which are necessary for maintaining good health.

In addition to this, the bacteria aid in guarding the digestive tract against pathogenic pathogens. According to several studies, kimchi has the potential to assist in the treatment of digestive conditions such as irritable bowel syndrome and inflammatory bowel disease.

In addition, kimchi is a rich source of probiotics, which are beneficial living bacteria that may be taken for their positive effects on one's health. It is well known that probiotics may strengthen the immune system, combat allergies, and encourage weight reduction. Including kimchi in your diet is, thus, a terrific approach to boosting the health of your digestive tract.

A good source of fiber: One serving of kimchi contains around 5 grams of fiber, making it a great supply of this essential nutrient. Fiber is a vital ingredient that plays a role in the regulation of digestion as well as the prevention of constipation. In addition, research has indicated that eating foods high in fiber can lower one's chance of developing heart disease as well as other chronic illnesses. Because of all of these benefits, including kimchi in your diet would be a wise decision.

Contains a good number of antioxidants*:* In addition to having a flavor all its own, kimchi also has a fair amount of antioxidants, which are substances that help prevent cell damage in the body and are found in many fruits and vegetables. It is believed that the antioxidants in kimchi are responsible for some of the health advantages linked with eating it, such as a reduced chance of developing cancer and a lower risk of blood pressure. Even while further studies are required to verify these results, there is little question that including kimchi in one's diet is not only beneficial but also tasty.

Because of all of these benefits, kimchi is an excellent meal to include in your diet, particularly if you are seeking methods to boost the health of your digestive tract. On the other hand, keep in mind that kimchi contains a lot of salt, thus eating it should only be done so in moderation at the very most. Please talk to a certified dietitian or your healthcare practitioner if you have any questions or concerns about having kimchi in your diet.

Use Cases of Kimchi for Health

Kimchi is a nutritious meal that possesses a wide range of advantageous properties for one's body. The following are some examples of how kimchi might benefit one's health:

Boost immunity*:* Kimchi is a traditional Korean meal that is made of fermented vegetables. It is known to be rich in vitamins A and C and can help strengthen the immune system. In addition to this, kimchi has been shown to contain lactic acid bacteria, which has been demonstrated to be beneficial to the immune system.

There is also evidence from a few studies that kimchi may be beneficial in warding off the common cold. Even though further study is required, the results of these studies show that including kimchi in your diet may be beneficial if you are seeking strategies to strengthen your immune system.

Improves digestion*:* The fermentation process that kimchi goes through not only lengthens the time that the meal can be stored, but also produces helpful microorganisms, which help the digestive process. Probiotics are living bacteria that, when taken, have the potential to provide several health advantages; one of these benefits is an improvement in digestion.

In addition, kimchi is an excellent source of fiber, which is known to have a role in maintaining regular bowel movements. Including kimchi in one's diet is a fantastic choice for individuals who are seeking a method to enhance their digestive health and who are looking for dietary options.

Lowers cholesterol levels: One of the most significant advantages of consuming kimchi is that it might assist in bringing about a reduction in one's cholesterol levels. This is because there are bacteria that produce lactic acid, which contributes to the breakdown of cholesterol. Additionally, kimchi is full of fiber, which is another factor that contributes to its ability to lower cholesterol levels. As a consequence of this, consuming kimchi as part of your diet is an excellent approach to maintaining a healthy cholesterol level.

Prevents cancer: Lactic acid bacteria are a type of probiotic bacteria that are typically found in fermented foods like kimchi. These bacteria have been shown to reduce the risk of developing cancer. The health of the stomach and the immune system can both be improved by these bacteria, which also have other beneficial effects on the body. In addition, there is evidence that bacteria that produce lactic acid can fight cancer.

According to several studies, these bacteria have the potential to impede the expansion and dissemination of cancer cells. In addition, lactic acid bacteria have been shown to stimulate the synthesis of chemicals in the body that inhibits the growth of tumors. As a consequence of this, kimchi has the potential to offer some protection against cancer. Nevertheless, to verify these effects, further study is required.

Controls blood sugar*:* Kimchi includes acetic acid, which has been demonstrated in studies to help enhance insulin sensitivity and control blood sugar levels. Acetic acid is also responsible for kimchi's ability to control blood sugar levels. As a consequence of this, consuming kimchi consistently may help to reduce rises in blood sugar after meals. Additionally, the probiotics included in kimchi have the potential to assist in lowering one's risk of acquiring type 2 diabetes.

Reduces inflammation*:* Kimchi is a healthful dish that offers various possible health advantages, despite having a strong flavor. One of these benefits is that it reduces inflammation. One of these advantages is its ability to lessen inflammation throughout the body. According to several studies, the probiotics included in kimchi can assist in the body's overall effort to decrease inflammation.

In addition, the fermentation process raises the levels of particular vitamins and minerals, which can also assist in reducing inflammation when present in sufficient quantities. As a consequence of this, kimchi has the potential to be an efficient natural therapy for illnesses that cause inflammation, such as arthritis and Crohn's disease.

Enhances cognitive function: There is some evidence that eating kimchi can have a beneficial influence on one's cognitive abilities. The high quantities of antioxidants and good microorganisms found in kimchi may be responsible for these advantageous benefits. Even though these findings need to be confirmed by more studies, eating kimchi may be a tasty method to improve brain function.

As has been demonstrated, the consumption of kimchi may provide a variety of positive effects on one's health. Try some kimchi if you're searching for something that's not only tasty but also good for your body and can help enhance your general health.

Health Benefits of Kimchi for Women

In recent years, kimchi has been more well-known as a nutritious dish because it contains a significant amount of various nutrients. The fermented cabbage dish known as kimchi is rich in beneficial nutrients including vitamins, minerals, and probiotics, making it a fantastic choice for women looking to improve their overall health. The consumption of kimchi is associated with several health advantages, some of which are listed below.

Weight loss: A recent study found that women who followed a diet that included kimchi were more likely to experience weight reduction than those who did not. Kimchi goes through a fermentation process that breaks down the carbs, which makes it simpler for the body to absorb and utilize carbohydrates as a source of energy. Because it is both high in fiber and low in calories, kimchi is an excellent dietary choice for people who are trying to reduce the amount of weight they are carrying.

Ladies who consumed kimchi daily over eight weeks were able to lose an average of five pounds. In addition to this, their levels of body fat and triglycerides were lower, but their levels of HDL cholesterol were much greater. Including kimchi in your diet may thus be an excellent place to begin if you are interested in reducing the amount of weight you are carrying.

Prevents yeast infection: One of the biggest advantages of kimchi is that it can help to prevent yeast infections. This is one of the many reasons why kimchi is so beneficial. The fermentation process results in the production of lactic acid, which contributes to the maintenance of an appropriate pH level in the vagina.

By doing so, you avoid an excess of yeast, which can otherwise cause an illness. In addition, there are a lot of beneficial probiotics in kimchi, which can also help keep yeast levels under control. As a consequence of this, consuming kimchi daily might assist in lowering one's likelihood of having a yeast infection.

Delays the aging process: The process of aging can be slowed down because kimchi, in addition to having a flavor all its own, is loaded with nutrients that aid to slow down the body's natural aging process. Kimchi, for instance, has a significant amount of free radical-fighting antioxidants as well as vitamins A, B, and C. Free radicals are one of the primary factors that contribute to the aging process, and the presence of these compounds helps to protect cells from the harm that may be caused by free radicals.

In addition, lactic acid, which has been demonstrated to enhance the skin's texture and help decrease the appearance of wrinkles, is present in kimchi. You might want to give kimchi a go if you're searching for a strategy to put off the effects of becoming older for as long as possible.

Potential Risks or Side Effects of Eating Kimchi

It is essential to be aware of the potential drawbacks of consuming kimchi even though it does have some positive effects on one's health, such as being an excellent source of probiotics. The following is a list of potential hazards or adverse reactions that may result from consuming kimchi.

Digestive issues: Because of the fermentation process that occurs during the making of kimchi, those who are not accustomed to consuming it may experience some stomach discomfort as a result of eating it. The fermentation process results in the production of gas and may also cause bloating, diarrhea, or constipation in some people. If you have never had kimchi before, it is recommended that you begin with a little amount and monitor how your body reacts to it.

High in sodium: Another possible concern associated with the kimchi diet is that it contains a lot of salt because of the kimchi. This is because salt water is used in the fermentation process of kimchi. If you have high blood pressure or are on a low-sodium diet, you should try to limit the amount of kimchi you consume. Kimchi contains a lot of sodium.

May contain bacteria: There is a possibility that the kimchi diet contains bacteria, which is another potential hazard of following such a regimen. This is because kimchi is a fermented food, and fermentation, in some cases, can result in the development of germs that are dangerous to humans. Consuming kimchi that has been heated and stored in the refrigerator can help reduce the risk of foodborne illness associated with eating raw kimchi.

Kimchi can be an addition to your diet that is both safe and beneficial if it is prepared and stored correctly. Before beginning to consume it, you should be aware of the possible dangers or negative effects it may have on your body. If you have any concerns, you should discuss them with either your primary care physician or a registered dietitian.

8-Step Guide to Making Kimchi at Home

Ingredients:

- 1 head of napa cabbage
- 1/2 cup of kosher salt
- 1/4 cup of sugar
- 1 tablespoon of grated ginger
- 3 cloves of garlic, minced
- 1/2 teaspoon of crushed red pepper flakes
- 1/4 cup of fish sauce
- 2 tablespoons of rice vinegar
- 1/2 cup of green onion

Step 1: Gather the ingredients.

The first thing that needs to be done to make kimchi is to gather all of the necessary components. This involves making sure you select the appropriate cabbage. Because there are many distinct varieties of cabbage, it is essential to pick one that will give your kimchi the ideal consistency and flavor profile. Young cabbages that are still soft and with leaves that are still crisp are ideal for making kimchi.

Step 2: Prepare the cabbage.

The next stage in creating kimchi is to prepare the cabbage, which you may do once you have acquired all of the necessary materials. You should begin by slicing the cabbage into very thin strips. This will be the first step. After that, combine the cabbage, salt, and water in a substantial dish. Check to see that the cabbage is completely covered in the saltwater combination before moving on. Put the bowl somewhere else and give it half an hour to settle. Because of this, the cabbage will become crispier and more delicious as a result of the salt's ability to suck moisture out of the cabbage. After thirty minutes, remove the cabbage from the water and give it a last rinsing in freshwater. Your cabbage is now prepared to be combined with the rest of the components for the kimchi.

Step 3: Make the kimchi paste.

Since this paste will act as the foundation for the flavor of your kimchi, you must take the time to develop a well-balanced concoction. To prepare a paste, put the following ingredients in a food processor: garlic, ginger, green onions, gochugaru (red pepper flakes), fish sauce, sugar, and water. After that, give the paste a taste, and based on what you find, modify the amounts of each ingredient so that it suits your preferences. After you have determined that the flavor of the paste meets your standards, you are ready to begin incorporating it into the cabbage.

Step 4: Add the kimchi paste to the cabbage.

The fourth step in the process of creating kimchi is to mix the cabbage with the kimchi paste. It is essential to completely work the kimchi paste into the cabbage leaves by massaging them together. This makes it more likely that each leaf will be uniformly covered and that the tastes will have an opportunity to combine. Wear gloves before rubbing the kimchi paste into the cabbage to avoid getting any of the paste on your hands. Because of the potential for the paste to be fairly hot, you should avoid letting it come into contact with your skin.

Step 5: Pack the kimchi into jars.

The final step in the process of manufacturing kimchi is to pack the finished product into jars. This is an essential stage in the process of making kimchi because it helps to keep the kimchi fresh and prevents the formation of germs. Before you use the jars to store the kimchi, you should make sure that they have been sterilized. This will help the kimchi retain its freshness for a longer period. Be careful to leave some room at the top of the jar while you are packing the kimchi, as this will allow for expansion when the kimchi is being stored.

Step 6: Ferment the kimchi.

Putting the finished kimchi into jars is the last stage in the process of creating kimchi. Because of this, the kimchi will be well-kept and have a longer shelf life than it would otherwise have. Be cautious to sterilize the jars before using them to avoid the kimchi from going bad. This may be done by boiling the jars in water for 10 minutes. After the kimchi has been packed into jars, put them in a place that is cold and dark and let them ferment for about a week or two. Check on them at regular intervals throughout this period to determine whether or not they have fermented to your satisfaction.

Step 7: Refrigerate the kimchi.

After the fermentation process is finished, go on to step seven, which is the chilling of the product. If you put your kimchi in the refrigerator, it will keep for up to four months. The fermentation process will proceed at a more leisurely pace as a result of this, which will assist to protect the kimchi's taste and texture.

Step 8: Serve and enjoy!

The eighth and final step of making kimchi is to serve and enjoy! Your preferred method of consumption for kimchi might vary greatly depending on how you choose to prepare it. It is versatile enough to be eaten on its own, with rice or noodles, as a side dish, as an appetizer, or even as a main course. You may also use kimchi as an ingredient in other recipes, such as kimchi fried rice or kimchi soup if you want to be creative and show off your culinary skills. No matter how you decide to consume it, homemade kimchi is a flavorful and nutritious way to amp up the heat of your meal.

3-Step Guide on How to Incorporate Kimchi Into Your Diet

The addition of savory kimchi to your dishes is not only tasty but also beneficial to your health. This traditional Korean meal is constructed of fermented vegetables and spices, and it may be utilized in a variety of contexts, such as a condiment, a side dish, or even as the main course. It has been demonstrated that eating kimchi may strengthen the immune system, improve digestion, and encourage weight reduction. Kimchi is rich in nutrients, probiotics, and antioxidants.

The following is a step-by-step instruction that will show you how to add kimchi to your diet in three easy steps, which will not only add flavor to your food but also enhance your overall health.

Step 1: Choose your kimchi.

Since there is such a wide variety of kimchi on the market, you should take some time to try out a few various kinds before settling on your preferred variety. There are many different varieties of kimchi, the most common of which is prepared with cabbage. However, there are additional variations made with radishes, carrots, turnips, and other vegetables. You may buy kimchi that is either mild or spicy, so select the kind that best suits your taste. If you follow the instructions in the previous article, you can also produce kimchi at home.

Step 2: Make kimchi a regular part of your diet.

After you've decided on the variety of kimchi you like most, it's time to start mixing it into the food you eat. Kimchi is a delicious addition to a wide variety of foods, including rice and noodle dishes, stews, curries, and stir-fries. Additionally, kimchi may be utilized as a topping for burgers or sandwiches, in addition to being utilized as a filler for dumplings or tacos. Put some thought into it, and see what kinds of foods you can concoct.

Step 3: Make sure you correctly store your kimchi.

When a jar of kimchi has been opened, it is essential to keep it appropriately to preserve its flavor and freshness. Always keep the kimchi in the refrigerator, and after each use, make sure the container is well-sealed before putting it away. Your kimchi will keep for a few weeks provided that it is stored properly.

Sample Recipes of Kimchi Dishes

Don't stress out if you don't have the time to create your kimchi! If you buy kimchi from a shop, you won't miss out on any of the health advantages of eating it because you won't have to make it yourself. The following is a selection of recipes to get you started:

Kimchi Fried Rice

This recipe for kimchi fried rice is the ideal way to utilize any remaining rice and kimchi in your fridge. For a dinner that is both savory and simple to prepare, the rice is stir-fried with kimchi, bacon, and green onions. You may use up any other unused veggies you have on hand by adding them to this kimchi fried rice dish and cooking them until they are tender.

Ingredients:

- 1 cup cooked rice
- 1/2 cup chopped kimchi
- 1/4 cup chopped bacon
- 1/4 cup diced green onion
- 1 tsp sesame oil
- 1 tbsp soy sauce
- 1 tsp rice vinegar
- 1/4 tsp black pepper

Instructions:

1. In a large pan set over medium heat, warm the oil from the sesame seeds.

2. To the skillet, add the rice that has been cooked, the kimchi, the bacon, and the green onion.

3. Stir the contents until they are completely combined and cooked thoroughly.

4. Stir the mixture once more after adding the soy sauce, rice vinegar, and ground black pepper.

5. To be served hot. Sunny-side-up egg and dried seaweed go very well with this dish.

Kimchi Pancakes

These pancakes are the ideal way to get your day started right. They have a wonderful taste and are loaded with a variety of beneficial elements. The instructions for the pancakes are straightforward, and the finished product is reliably mouthwatering.

Ingredients:

- 1 cup kimchi, finely chopped
- 1/2 cup all-purpose flour
- 1/2 cup rice flour
- 1 teaspoon baking powder
- 1/4 teaspoon salt
- 1 egg, beaten
- 1/4 cup milk
- 2 tablespoons vegetable oil, plus more for frying

Instructions:

1. In a large mixing basin, combine the kimchi, rice flour, all-purpose flour, baking powder, and salt.

2. After adding the egg and milk, be sure to thoroughly blend the ingredients.

3. In a frying pan, bring the vegetable oil up to temperature over medium heat.

4. Put one-fourth of a cup of the batter into the pan, and cook it for two to three minutes on each side, or until it is golden brown.

5. Prepare with the toppings of your choice and serve.

Spicy Kimchi Noodles

Spicy Kimchi Noodles are a dish that can be created in a matter of minutes and are both quick and simple to prepare. This dish is ideal for folks who enjoy spicy foods because it mixes the spiciness of kimchi with the creaminess of noodles to create a dish that is bursting with flavor. In addition, it calls for basic ingredients, which are readily available in the kitchens of most people, making it an excellent choice for supper throughout the week.

Ingredients:

- 8 oz. dry noodles
- 1/2 cup kimchi, chopped
- 1/4 cup onion, chopped
- 1 tbsp. olive oil
- 1 tsp. garlic, minced
- salt, and pepper, to taste

Instructions:

1. Prepare the noodles by the directions on the package. Drain, then put it to the side.

2. In a large skillet, heat olive oil over medium heat. Add onions and sauté until transparent.

3. After adding the kimchi and the garlic, continue to simmer for an additional two to three minutes, or until the kimchi is hot throughout.

4. Place the cooked noodles in the skillet, then add the remaining ingredients and mix until everything is incorporated. Salt and pepper can be added to taste as a seasoning. To be served hot.

Kimchi Soup

Enjoying a classic Korean soup in the form of this kimchi soup recipe is the ideal method to do it. To prepare this dish, kimchi is first boiled in a broth with other ingredients, including tofu, mushrooms, and scallions. The end product is a savory and filling soup that can be consumed at any time of year due to its versatility.

Ingredients:

- 1-quart vegetable broth
- 4 cups kimchi, chopped
- 1 block of tofu, cut into cubes
- 8-10 mushrooms, sliced
- 3 green onions, thinly sliced

Instructions:

1. The vegetable broth should be brought to a boil in a big saucepan.
2. Include kimchi, tofu, mushrooms, and scallions in the dish. Maintain a low simmer for around 10–15 minutes, or until everything is well warmed.
3. Serve while still hot, and enjoy!

Braised Pork with Kimchi

Kimchi stew is a popular Korean food, and another famous Korean dish is braised pork with kimchi. These two dishes are similar, however braised pork with kimchi is somewhat different. The meal is prepared by first braising pork belly in kimchi broth, then cooking the pork belly in a mixture that includes gochujang, garlic, ginger, and green onion. As a consequence, you will end up with a piece of beef that is tasty, soft and works wonderfully with rice and other side dishes.

Ingredients:

- 1 pound pork belly, cut into 1-inch cubes
- 1 tablespoon gochujang
- 1 tablespoon garlic, minced
- 1 tablespoon ginger, minced
- 1 green onion, thinly sliced
- 4 cups kimchi, chopped
- 3 cups chicken stock
- 1 teaspoon sesame oil
- 1 teaspoon salt
- 1 teaspoon black pepper

Instructions:

1. Cubes of pork belly, gochujang, garlic, ginger, and chopped green onion should be combined in a Dutch oven or another big saucepan. Mixing will be easier if you stir.

2. Bring the kimchi and the chicken stock to a boil after adding them.

3. Turn the heat down to low and simmer the mixture for one hour.

4. To season, add some salt, black pepper, and toasted sesame oil.

5. To be served hot. When served with rice and various side dishes, it tastes the best.

Korean Kimchi Chicken

This recipe for Korean Kimchi Chicken is a fantastic way to enjoy a dinner that is both nutritious and full of flavor. The chicken receives its robust taste from a marinade consisting of Korean kimchi, gochujang, soy sauce, and sugar. This process imparts the chicken with the flavors. The kimchi not only helps to tenderize the chicken but also contributes to the bird's incredible amount of juice.

After that, the chicken is pan-fried until it attains a golden brown and crispy texture. Complete the dinner by accompanying it with steamed rice and a variety of veggies. This dish is also wonderful for meal prep; simply multiply the ingredients by two or three, and you'll have enough food to last you through the week.

Ingredients:

- 1 pound boneless, skinless chicken breasts, cut into thin strips
- 1 cup kimchi, roughly chopped
- 2 tablespoons gochujang
- 3 tablespoons soy sauce
- 3 tablespoons sugar
- 1 tablespoon vegetable oil
- 1/2 teaspoon sesame oil
- steamed rice and vegetables, for serving

Instructions:

1. Combine the kimchi, gochujang, soy sauce, sugar, vegetable oil, and sesame oil in a large bowl and whisk until smooth. After adding the chicken strips, evenly cover them with the marinade and set aside. Relax the pressure for at least half an hour and up to a full day.

2. Cook the chicken strips in a large pan over medium-high heat until they are golden brown and cooked through, which should take around 5-7 minutes on each side. Rice and steamed veggies should be served on the side.

Kimchi Fried Egg

This Kimchi Fried Egg dish is a delicious way to get your day started on the right foot. For a savory and wholesome meal, the eggs are fried in a pan and then topped with kimchi and scallions once they have finished cooking.

Ingredients:

- 1 teaspoon oil
- 4 eggs
- 1/4 cup kimchi, diced
- 1 scallion, thinly sliced
- hot sauce, if desired

Instructions:

1. In a bowl, whisk together the eggs and the liquid from the kimchi.

2. In a big pan that is set over medium-high heat, warm up one teaspoon of oil. After adding the eggs, continue to simmer for about two minutes, or until the whites have solidified but the yolks have retained their liquid consistency.

3. Cook for a further one to two minutes after adding the kimchi and onions, or until the kimchi has reached the desired temperature. Immediately serve with rice and spicy sauce on the side, if preferred. Enjoy!

Kimchi Quesadilla

This recipe for Kimchi Quesadillas strikes the ideal balance between savory and spicy flavors. The meltiness of the cheese, the crispiness of the tortilla, and the spiciness of the kimchi combine to produce a quesadilla that is not only tasty but also quite simple to prepare. The fact that this dish can be prepared from start to finish in only a quarter of an hour is easily the most appealing aspect of the given recipe. This Kimchi Quesadilla Recipe is exactly what you need if you are in the mood for a supper that is both easy to prepare and delicious.

Ingredients:

- 4 large tortillas
- 1 cup kimchi, chopped
- 1 cup shredded cheddar cheese
- 1/2 teaspoon garlic powder
- Salt and pepper, to taste

Instructions:

1. To begin, set your oven's temperature to 350 degrees as it preheats. The kimchi should be cooked over medium heat in a big pan until it is pliable and has a little browning on the edges. After the kimchi has finished cooking, place it in a bowl and put it aside.

2. After that, in the same skillet, fry the bacon over medium heat until it reaches a crisp consistency. After

the bacon has been cooked, transfer it to a platter that has been lined with paper towels so that it may cool.

3. Now comes the fun part: putting together the quesadillas! To begin, divide the kimchi into four equal portions and put them on each tortilla. After that, place a quarter cup of cheese and two slices of bacon on top of each tortilla. At this point, you will want to take each tortilla and fold it in half before placing it on a baking sheet that has been lined with parchment paper.

4. Quesadillas should be baked for ten to twelve minutes, or until they have a golden brown color and the cheese has melted. Enjoy this dish with some sour cream on the side!

Kimchi Grilled Cheese Sandwich

This recipe for kimchi grilled cheese sandwiches is the ideal way to break up the monotony of your typical lunchtime routine. A sandwich that is both savory and satisfying is created when thick bread, mozzarella cheese, and spicy kimchi are combined. Plus, kimchi provides a natural supply of probiotics, which can assist to enhance your immune system.

Ingredients:

- 1/2 cup kimchi, drained
- 1/4 cup mozzarella cheese, shredded
- 2 slices bread
- 1 tablespoon butter

Instructions:

1. Heat a skillet over medium heat.
2. Slather one side of each slice of bread with butter.
3. Arrange the bread in the skillet with the buttered side facing down.
4. Spread some kimchi on the toast, then sprinkle some mozzarella cheese on top.
5. Put the top slice of bread on the buttered side and use it to seal the sandwich.

6. Cook for about three minutes per side, or until the cheese is melted and golden brown, whichever comes first.

Kimchi Dumplings Recipe

These kimchi dumplings are the perfect way to enjoy the unique flavor of kimchi in a bite-sized snack.

Ingredients:

- 1/2 pound ground pork
- 1/4 teaspoon salt
- 1/4 teaspoon black pepper
- 1 cup chopped kimchi
- 1 teaspoon sesame oil
- 1 tablespoon sugar
- Dumpling wrappers
- Water for sealing dumplings

Instructions:

1. Mix kimchi, ground pork, salt, pepper, sugar, and sesame oil in a bowl until everything is well distributed. Combine well and then set aside.

2. To begin putting together the dumplings, take one of the wrappers and set it in the palm of your hand. Wet the edges of the wrapper with your fingertips that have been dipped in water.

3. Place approximately one heaping tablespoon's worth of the kimchi mixture in the middle of the wrapper.

4. Wrap the filling in the wrapper by bringing the corners of the wrapper up around it and ensuring sure the filling is completely enclosed. To ensure that the edges are completely enclosed, pinch them together.

5. Repeat the process with the rest of the wrappers and the filling.

6. You have the option of either frying or steaming the dumplings until they are completely cooked through once they have been wrapped. Enjoy them with a dipping sauce made of soy sauce and vinegar that you serve beside them.

Conclusion

The topography and history of Korea have had a significant influence on the development of the country's cuisine, which is characterized by an unusual combination of sweet, sour, and savory tastes. The robust flavors and vivid hues that characterize Korean cuisine are what make it famous across the world, from the spiciness of kimchi to the finesse of jeon.

Women in Korea have been the ones responsible for maintaining the country's culinary traditions for many years. Men have only just started becoming involved in the cooking process in recent decades. Because of this, there is a major emphasis on using healthful and nutrient-dense foods in Korean cuisine.

The lush soil of Korea is used in the preparation of many Korean cuisines, which call for the use of fresh vegetables. To make delectable soups and stews, herbs and spices are very commonly employed. Rice is an essential component of the Korean diet and is frequently consumed alongside other foods such as meat and fish. The proliferation of Korean restaurants all over the world can be attributed to the rising popularity of

Korean gastronomy. These restaurants provide customers with the opportunity to enjoy the distinctive flavor of Korean cuisine.

One of the most well-liked Korean cuisines is kimchi, which is a dish consisting of spicy fermented cabbage. It is common practice to use it as a supplementary dish or as a component in other preparations. Fermentation of cabbage and other vegetables in a combination of chili peppers, salt, and garlic is the process that gives kimchi its distinctive flavor. Beneficial microorganisms that support healthy digestion are produced as a byproduct of this fermentation process.

A wide range of meals can benefit from the addition of kimchi due to its adaptability as an ingredient. This fermented cabbage dish may be found in a wide variety of cuisines, including kimchi dumplings, kimchi fried rice, and kimchi soup, to name just a few of them. A flavorful kick may also be given to salads and sandwiches by including kimchi in the mix.

Including kimchi in one's diet is associated with several positive health effects, particularly for women. Vitamins A and C may be found in healthy amounts in kimchi. Kimchi is popular for its flavor as well as its numerous positive effects on one's health. It is commonly acknowledged that kimchi has the power to strengthen one's immune system. The probiotics in kimchi can aid in the fight against pathogenic bacteria and enhance the health of the digestive tract. In addition, kimchi is an excellent source of antioxidants, which are substances that help the body defend itself against cellular damage. Additionally contributing to better skin health are the vitamins and minerals found in kimchi.

Kimchi is an excellent choice to take into consideration if you would want to enhance the flavor of your diet. You may eat kimchi on its own or include it in a variety of other recipes. In addition to being simple to prepare at home, it is a scrumptious and wholesome method for spicing up your meals.

FAQ

What is kimchi?

Kimchi is a traditional Korean dish made of fermented vegetables, typically cabbage and radish, with a variety of seasonings.

How is kimchi made?

Kimchi is made by fermenting vegetables in a mixture of water, salt, and spices. The vegetables are typically left to ferment for several weeks or months.

What are the benefits of kimchi?

Kimchi is a good source of vitamins A and C, as well as fiber and probiotics. Additionally, the fermentation process creates beneficial compounds that can help to improve digestive health.

Are there any risks associated with eating kimchi?

If kimchi is not prepared properly, it can contain harmful bacteria that can cause food poisoning. However, this risk can be minimized by ensuring that kimchi is made with fresh, clean ingredients and stored properly.

How should kimchi be stored?

Kimchi should be stored in an airtight container in the refrigerator. It will continue to ferment over time, so it should be consumed within 1-2 months for the best quality.

Can kimchi be frozen?

Yes, kimchi can be frozen for long-term storage. However, it may become mushy when thawed and the flavor may change somewhat.

How long does kimchi last?

Homemade kimchi will last up to 4 months in the refrigerator or up to 6 months in the freezer.

What are some common ways to eat kimchi?

Kimchi can be eaten on its own or as an ingredient in other dishes such as rice, noodles, or soup.

Where can I buy kimchi?

Kimchi is widely available in Asian markets and some grocery stores. It can also be ordered online from specialty retailers.

References and Helpful Links

"9 Surprising Benefits of Kimchi." Healthline, 14 Jan. 2021, https://www.healthline.com/nutrition/benefits-of-kimchi.

10 Benefits Of Kimchi. https://woop.co.nz/blog/post/10-benefits-of-kimchi. Accessed 25 Nov. 2022.

Cabbage, Kimchi Nutrition Facts and Analysis. https://www.nutrition-value.org/Cabbage%2C_kimchi_nutritional_value.html. Accessed 25 Nov. 2022.

Kim, Eun Kyoung, et al. "Fermented Kimchi Reduces Body Weight and Improves Metabolic Parameters in Overweight and Obese Patients." Nutrition Research (New York, N.Y.), vol. 31, no. 6, June 2011, pp. 436–43. PubMed, https://doi.org/10.1016/j.nutres.2011.05.011.

"Kimchi Can Add Some Spice To Everything From Eggs To Burgers, And You Should Definitely Be Eating It." Women's Health, 19 Apr. 2021, https://www.womenshealthmag.com/food/a29892608/health-benefits-of-kimchi.

Larbi, Miranda. "How to Make Kimchi: 20-Minute Recipe by The Gut Stuff." Stylist, 20 Sept. 2022, https://www.stylist.co.uk/fitness-health/food/how-to-make-kimchi/708654.

"Noom vs. Weight Watchers: Which Diet Is Better for You?" LIVESTRONG.COM, https://www.livestrong.com/article/13726897-noom-vs-weight-watchers/. Accessed 25 Nov. 2022.

Sue. "Kimchi Jjim (Braised Kimchi)." My Korean Kitchen, 28 Mar. 2020, https://mykoreankitchen.com/kimchi-jjim-braised-kimchi/.

"The History of Kimchi, Everyone's Favorite Side Dish." KORELIMITED, https://korelimited.com/blogs/korelimited/the-history-of-kimchi-everyone-s-favorite-side-dish. Accessed 25 Nov. 2022.